# Rhythms of the Heart

### by

## Christal Nicole Traylor

Bloomington, IN    authorHOUSE    Milton Keynes, UK

AuthorHouse™
1663 Liberty Drive, Suite 200
Bloomington, IN 47403
www.authorhouse.com
Phone: 1-800-839-8640

AuthorHouse™ UK Ltd.
500 Avebury Boulevard
Central Milton Keynes, MK9 2BE
www.authorhouse.co.uk
Phone: 08001974150

First published by AuthorHouse 4/24/2006

ISBN: 1-4259-1799-2 (sc)

Printed in the United States of America
Bloomington, Indiana

This book is printed on acid-free paper.

To the God, I give all glory and praises. I will forever praise him for the talents and blessings that he has and will continuously bestow upon me.

# Acknowledgments

I want to give thanks first of all to God, because without him, I could do nothing. I'd like to thank Necoma, my beautiful love child, for being a light and inspiration with his undying, innocent, and pure unconditional love. I'd like to thank my mother and father and sisters for their love, beauty and spirituality. I believe that all things happen in our lives for a reason, so I'd also like to thank all of the lost loves in my life. The pain and sorrow that I've felt has helped to make this happen.

# Contents

*Love*

# For My Son

How can I express the way I feel
　　　for this child of mine
So lovely and so beautiful, I'll love him
　　　throughout time

His smile, his laugh, the way he plays
He brightens up every day
A kiss, a hug, and tickles too
I'll love him in every way

# He Belongs to Another

Heart
What are you doing?
This man you love
        is not yours.

Mind
What are you thinking?
Forget this man
        who belongs to another.

Lips
What are you speaking?
Do not say
        she deserves him not.

Man
Where is your double?
You are what
        I've been longing for.

# Fountain of My Love

If you could drink from the fountain of my love you would find
A love so sweet and a taste to divine

My waters run slow and smooth and clear
No poisons to be found, so there's nothing to fear

Take a sip from my fountain of love and you'll sigh
To finally have found that ultimate high

Saturate yourself in the pools of my fountain
Where you can find joy and no sorrow again

Just drink, take a sip, dive into my love
A fountain ever-flowing, this fountain of my love

# Help Me

My body is chilled.
Can you help me?
Wrap me in your warmth.
Shield the light.
I shall lie upon your shoulder,
and rest through the night.

My heart is empty.
Can you help me, please?
Fill me with your love.
Give me an inner peace.
My love will be yours,
and it shall never cease.

# I Can't

I can't sleep,
    because I'm dreaming of you.
Dreaming of how it will be in time
Fantasizing of our days together

I can't think,
    because I'm thinking of you.
Thinking of the love you make me feel
Wondering if you're feeling the same way too

Every dream is made up of you
What I want to be with you
Every thought consists of you
What I need and yearn from you

I can't cry,
    because I'm crying for you.
Crying for you to come back home
Mourning because you left me alone

I can't feel,
    because I'm feeling for you
Feeling emotions kept hidden inside
Touching those things that remind me of you

Every tear is shed for you
What makes you do the things you do
Every feeling is caused by you
What makes me feel the way I do?

# Infatuation

Another sweet letter you've sent to me
Proclaiming the love that you feel
And I want desperately to share your feelings
But my heart warns me not to yield

More soft words you whisper in my ear
Announcing you'll always be true
But my mind tells me not to listen
'Cause these words you speak, they are not new

A dozen roses arrive by the hour
Tempting me to be your love
And I would if I could, if I could
But infatuation, is not the same as love

# Love

Love can be a sickness,
    Weakening the body and hurting it,
    Plaguing the mind with thoughts of lust,
    Plaguing the mind...
    Love.

Love can be a beautiful flower,
    A wonderful gift,
    Growing more beautiful with everyday that passes,
    Growing more beautiful...
    Love.

Love can be a venomous snake,
    Slithering, slowly through the body,
    Squeezing the heart and biting the skin,
    Poisoning the hands with touch,
    Poisoning the hands...
    Love.

Love can be the dawn of morning,
    Bright, radiant and new,
    Creating a bond between two people,
    Creating a bond...
    Love.
    Between two people...
    Love.

# Love Bug

boy
girl
I couldn't see our face to tell
your hands or body shape at al
whatever it was you could've been
I never saw it to begin

could you have
would you have
loved me and been the friend I need
there to take care of me when I am old
would you share you blanket when I am cold

why
what reason
you bit me and infected me
confusing me and scaring me
rejecting me- I rejected you
will you be back in time

# Love Poison

It's interesting, the effect of this thing called love
Stronger than the strongest man, it weakens
Wilder than the wildest beast, it runs
Deeper than the depths of the sea, it goes

Lips that speak lies, are yearned to be kissed
Hands that yield nothing, are longed to be held

So you see the effect that you've had on me, love
Where once I was strong, you've made me weak
Stolen is the breath of live you gave
Returned has the thirst that you quenched

A heart that beats empty, cries out to be filled
A body that lies lonely, desires to be held

A bittersweet poison it is, this love
So much joy does it give, much more does it take
It has the power to lift, the power to drown
So sweet, the injection, so bitter, the extraction

# More Than Just Words

Some say "I love you" without any thought
    As if it means nothing
    As if it's just words
But "I love you," to me, is more than just words
    Within each word is a different meaning
    Within each word is a different feeling
I, am the one who loved you last night
    The one who touched you
    The one you held
Love, is the feeling deep down in my heart
    The chill on my skin
    The fire you've ignited
You, are the man I dream of in sleep
    I run to in sadness
    I kiss in the darkness
Some say "I love you" without any thought
    As if it means nothing
    As if it's just words
But "I love you," to me, is more than just words
    More than just words, it is to me
    To me, it is more than just words.

# My Love

Depression and sorrow
        You've brought me from
And I know that you'll always
        Be
        My Love.

When the road seems dark
        And lonely to me
You're my guiding light
        And I see
        My Love.

My Love,
You make me feel like I'm flying,
        I'm free
And no one could ever take you from me.

My love,
        You are my first and only
                True Love.

# My, My, My- A love poem

My sunrise
     that's what you are
A constant light
     shining in my heart
Waking me up
     to pleasures unknown
Opening my eyes
     to things unseen
Giving me love
     that's never been given.

My sunset
     every time you leave me
Taking away
     the light in my eyes
Draining the substance
     within my heart
Leaving me wanting
     for your love.

My love
     that's who you are
Impregnated with love
     when you are near
A million deaths
     when you're away.

My guiding light
My evening sun
You are-
     My love for life.

# Question Is

Is it really okay
        for me to love you this way
To allow my heart these feelings

Is it permissible for me
        to hand over the key
To my heart, my body and my life

Can you tell me if it's right
        to stay up all night
Thinking of how it would be if you were here

Can you tell me if I should submit
        to this passion no one permits
Flooding my dreams and realities

Is it really allowed
        to have my head in this cloud
Of love and joy and happiness

Should I follow my heart
        and let you be a part
Of a love once thought not to be real

# Set Me Free

Like a caged bird wanting to be free
Free to sing
Free to fly
That is my love
Set it free

Like a black bear imprisoned by man
Restrained by walls
Controlled by barriers
That is my heart
Set it free

Like a beautiful flower mistaken for a weed
Stomped under foot
Uprooted from the ground
This is my body
Set me free

# That Moment

All I want is a moment with you
To be with you
To share with you

A moment to tell you what's on my mind
And show you what's in my heart

All I need is a piece of time
To mold for you
To shape for you

A piece of time made just for us
To do with whatever we please

All I desire is that moment together
To give to you
To yield to you

And it is at that moment, my love
We shall know what is true

# True Beauty

You stare into my eyes and are mesmerized
    By the beauty that lies within them
But true beauty is in the way I look at you
    Seeing you for the man you really are
    I'll never judge you, I'll always accept you
    A unique greatness that I can truly see

You long for my lips and their fullness
    The kisses of sweetness and honey
But you fail to see that their true beauty
    Is the honesty that flows from within them
    Speaking of truths and no fabrications
    My words you always can trust

So beautiful to you is the smoothness of my legs
    And you love how they wrap all around you
But true beauty, my love, is how they walk beside you
    Never leaving your side in times of trouble
    Trusting the path that you've chosen for us
    Believing you won't lead us astray

You hold my body and sigh at its warmth
    So lovely you believe are its curves
True beauty is the body that belongs to one man
    That lies beside you at every day's end
    A beauty that shows from deep within
    True beauty is the woman in me.

# Spiritual

# Crazy Weather

Crazy weather we're having, you say
Lightning and thunder rumbling in the sky
Rain pounding upon the ground
as the sun shines brightly above

Crazy weather we're having, you think
Sunny days and snowy nights
Cold today and hot tomorrow
Crazy, crazy weather

The signs of the time are showing, I say
That God is sure to come
Taking back the elite few
and leaving behind all others

The signs of the time are showing, I think
Won't you look around and see
He said in his Word that he's coming again
I'm reading it loud and clear

Crazy weather, you say and think
But I say it's the signs of the time

# Dear Lord

Distress signal-
	I'm sending out
I'm hoping that you can see the signs
As the light from the lighthouse cuts thru the fog
I'm praying my signal comes thru

Heartbroken-
	I'm crying out
I'm desiring an answer from you
As a baby's cry reaches a mother
I'm praying my plea finds your ear

Lord, please hear my cry tonight-
	As I fall on my knees to pray
I pray that you keep me from drowning in fear
I pray you'll relieve my pain
Send down your power of deliverance, Lord
Deliver me from guilt and shame

Pressure-
	Deep inside of me
I'm feeling my chest will explode
As the morning dew dries, with the rising of the sun
I'm praying the pressure will ease

Emptiness-
        Consumes me daily
I feel as though I'm falling into darkness
As the flower breaks thru the ground and blooms
I'm praying you'll shed light on my day
Lord, please hear my plea tonight-
        As I fall on my face to pray
I pray that you mend my broken heart
I pray you'll supply my needs
Send down your power of love, my Lord
Dear Lord, to you do I pray

# Happiness

Night and Day
What is the difference?
No matter what time it is,
      I'm thinking of you.

When I wake up in the morning,
      I'm thinking of you.
When I'm driving down the street,
      My thoughts may wonder
      And I ask this question-
      Where are you?

You call yourself happiness,
      Yet all I feel is confusion,
There's a yearning inside of me
      But I feel so fulfilled.

You've done this
You've made me forget
      All of those little simple things.

I've forgotten my worries
I've forgotten my pains
Because of you
Oh, wonderful happiness.

# Him

I worry greatly about the children of today.
Protected shortly by a mother's arms.

The little girls who play in mom's pearls.
The little boys with the He-Man toys.

Through all of my fears, I shed not a tear.
For I know someone who protects them all.

He protects them through winter,
He protects them through spring,
He even protects them through summer and fall.

He is the almighty God.
        Yes, Almighty
For there is no one above him.

What can he do?
        He can do all things
HE can do all things but fail.

# Lead me, Lord

Because I love you with all of my heart,
      I will serve you with it.

I will look to you for my guidance
      my instruction and my strength

You are a light when everything seems dark
      A guide when I can not see my way

Use me Lord for whatever you want
      Your work I will do without hesitation

Everyday you bless me with life, health & strength
      I could never re-pay your love & kindness

Guide my footsteps on the path of righteousness
      Wash me, cleanse me & make me whole.

# Lord I Need You

My heart is aching
     And I feel so alone
          Lord I need you to help me go on

My heart is sad
     And no one is true
          Lord I need you to show me what to do

You are my light
     My Joy
          My Happiness
My heart is longing
     Lord I need you to fulfill

# Perfect Love

searching for love in every wrong place
I felt I'd never be complete
seeking for kindness where no one should
I thought that I had no place...
when I gave you my hand and you gave me yours
I knew I had not gone wrong
from the moment you told me- I'll never leave
I knew that it had to be true...
you've given me love without conditions
a promise of life everlasting
you've given me peace in the midst of storms
and light in the midnight hour
perfect love
from a perfect God
to an imperfect person like me

# Picture This

Picture a star
Shining so bright
Shining so bright, it can't go unnoticed

Three men
Three wise men
Wise men bringing gifts for a king

Picture a manger
With cows and horses
Hay and straw all around

One baby
A mother and a father
Kneeling admiring their child

Picture yourself
The mother of this child
A girl with not many years

Feel the love
Feel the joy
The fear that hangs in the air

Picture this
And know the meaning
When Jesus was born, the King

# Sweet Jesus

So much joy you've given to me
You've taken away every misery
The pain and sorrow I'd felt before
Have been washed away, so I feel no more
It's truly the sweetest sense of fulfillment
To have your feelings of sentiment
Your love and kindness draw me nearer to you
You've cleansed my heart and made me brand new
It's insane to believe that I could ever live
Without the peace and happiness that only you can give
Sweet Jesus you are and will always be
Allow me in your presence, throughout eternity

# The Ragged Man

His outside appearance
       is very ragged.
His clothes are soiled,
His hair is matted,
      but there's something about
         his presence.

Look into his glazed eyes,
      There are treasures to be found.
Dip into the cool waters of his soul,
      And cleanse your dirty thoughts.

This ragged man,
      With soiled clothing and matted hair,
Is cleaner than you or me.

# The Story

She came in
    and immediately-
        it was different.

She shed tears of joy,
    and tears of happiness,
        and she even shed tears of excitement.

She was one of God's messengers-
    there to tell a story.

A story so harmonic,
    my ears still tingle.
A story so vivid,
    I see it before me.

God gave her a message,
    A story, I call it.
        A story so old,
            that's preached ev'ry Sunday.

God opened my eyes,
    so that I might see.
He opened my ears,
    so that I might hear

And for the first time,
    I heard-
        The Story.

# The Wiry Man

You can't sit me down
     It's the spirit
You can't shut me up
     It's the Lord

Satan!
I rebuke you
You're out of my life
I don't need you

You can't hurt me
     It's the spirit
You can't bring me down
     It's the Lord

Satan!
I rebuke you
You're out of my life
I don't need you.

# Unexplainable

the way you love me, even when I'm wrong
the way you hold me, even when I've turned
the way you remember me, even when I've forgotten

it's just unexplainable

to know that you're there- leading and guiding
to know that  you'll stay- watching and providing
it's just unexplainable, the way that you are...

I guess that's the reason why-
we call you GOD.

# You Blessed My Heart

I sat there
      and I listened
I listened so closely
      it hurt me
It hurt me so badly
it broke me

The words that you spoke

You tore me
You tore me to shreds
      But you blessed me
You stomped on my feet
      But you blessed me

# You have Love

I have nothing,
    You have Love.

I have hatred,
    You have Love.

My life is filled with loneliness,
    And You,
        My Lord,
            Have Love.

People mock and scorn me each day,
    But You,
        My Lord,
            Have Love.

I want to be even more like you,
    Because You,
        Dear Lord,
            Have Love.

# Pain and Sorrow

# A Promise to Me

Last night-
      I lay here waiting,
      But never satisfied.
Do what you want,
      Do what you please,
But never break a promise to me.

My ears tingled-
      What you said,
      But never showed.
Say what you will,
      Say what you like,
But never break a promise to me.

Goose bumps-
      The way you touched me,
      But never meant.
Act how you may,
      Act how you might,
But never break a promise to me.

For a promise tome,
      Is a promise to keep.
If never to any,
      Keep your promise to me.

# Alone

I must be
Must be
Alone

No love can suit me
Comfort me
Touch me

I must be
Need to be
Be
Alone

I need a love that can wait
For me-Patiently
'til I unite with it...

Slowly.

Gradually.

So, until then...

I must be
Need to be
Have to be
Be
Alone

# Can You Believe It?

There's so much I want to say,
So many things I want to tell you,
I am afraid...
        Can you believe it?

Many people do not understand.
Everyone, even I, gets lonely sometimes.

I am so shy...
        Can you believe it?
I can not express my feelings the way I want to...

If only I could...

Then I would get close, very close
Whisper my feelings,
        and seal them with a kiss.

But I can't do that,
        And I lose some of the things I want...
                Can you believe it?

# Confusion

It seems as though,
　　I'm all alone

One dot, on a sheet of paper

Surrounded by things
　　I don't understand
Saturated by feelings
　　I can't express...

I sometimes wonder,
　　Where he is

One man, in a circle of love

Waiting to accept me
　　Into his heart
Wanting to fulfill
　　My utmost desires...

I can't stop the tears,
　　That run down my cheek

One woman, lying in bed

Crying out, because
        I can't find my love
Hating my heart, because
        It won't accept him...

It seems as though,
        I need too much

One arm, stretched to receive

A hand to touch
        In times of despair
Lips that form
        Announcing "I Need You"

# Dream Lost and Found

Once I dreamed of being somebody
A person of stature and respect...
Somebody my children could smile and look up to
Somebody of whom her parents would be proud

I dreamed I had beauty, grace and dignity
A woman whose presence astounded...
Somebody who turned the heads of mankind
Somebody who could not be ignored

I dreamed I was somebody who had possessions
A person with love, joy and peace...
Somebody whose happiness lit up the room
Somebody who showed no pain

What happens to all of the dreams you lose?
The dreams you don't feel will come true...
Surely there's a place to retrieve all dreams
Could there be a dream lost and found?

# Friendless

Yeah, we laughed and talked and spent time together
And all the time you were eyeing my man
Laughing, and calling me a fool behind my back
A fool indeed, because I called you friend
Believing that finally, I had a confidant
Of course, I wouldn't tell you everything
You're still a woman, a human being
Not to be trusted until much time has passed
Remember when you cried and seemed so concerned
You told me "Don't scare me like that ever again"
What was all that
Some plot to destroy me
You must think I'm stupid
Some fly in your trap
Waiting to be drained of all life
You know, you are good
You really had me fooled
So close to the edge
In your hands I could've fallen
But I'm glad I woke up
You see, I was dreaming
Believe me, I'll never dream that again
Content with my loneliness
And a lock on my heart
That's how you have to be
When you're friendless

# How I Really Feel

It's not real
None of it is real
This smile you see upon my face
     Is only hiding the frown
     The look of sadness
         Of how I really feel

It's not real, I tell you
No, nothing you see is real
This laughter you hear coming from my throat
     Is only hiding the whimpers
     The sounds of crying
         Of how I really feel

It truly is not real
Not one bit of it is real
This sparkle you think you see in the corner of my
eye
     Is only hiding the darkness
     The emptiness inside
         Of how I really feel

It's not real, I say
The things that you see
     The joy, the happiness displayed
It is not real
The things you hear
     The laughter, and sweet songs in the air

It's not real
None of it is real
None of it is the way I really feel...

# I Cheated on You

Yes, I cheated on you
      Even as harsh as it is
He kissed me
He touched me
But you must know
      I stopped it at that

These lips of mine
      were not his to touch
This skin could never be his

I did you wrong
      and now you're gone
I deserve that
      and I love you still.

# I Don't Understand

I don't understand how you treat me

Telling me you love me
      And care for me so
Saying that you'll be there
      And always be true
While going back to her
      And proclaiming the same

I don't understand why I lie to myself

Telling myself to wait
      And be patient
Saying that you love me
      And no one else more
While my soul contradicts me
      And knows not your name

# I Never Meant to Hurt You

If only you would listen,
     Listen to my words.
If only you would hear me out,
     Hear the things I say.

You would know,
     I never meant to hurt you.

If only you could see the pain,
     See the pain I feel.
If only you could hear my thoughts,
     Then you'd hear how I'm thinking of you.

And you would know,
     I never meant to hurt you.

# I Should Have Let You Go

I knew it the first time that we met
that something was amiss
It wasn't in the way you smiled
        or even in your kiss
I knew that I should let you go
        but passion wouldn't permit

The days and nights I spent with you
        not knowing how to be free
You never thought to let me go
        I was the only one who didn't see
I knew that I should let you go
        before it was too late

I thought that I could fill your void
        when first you touched my hand
But now I know I did the right thing
        that night I took a stand
I knew that I should let you go
        to free my misery

# I Vowed

From the moment I saw him
    I knew he was the one.

I love the way he walked,
    The way he talked,
    The way he said my name...

And I vowed that from that day forward-
    I would love him until  the end.

He never said he loved me,
    But I could see it in his eyes.
He never said he cared for me,
    But I could hear it in his voice.

And when friends told me he was seeing another-
    I knew they were telling me lies.

My man was faithful,
    And loyal,
    And true,
He would never do anything to hurt me...

The first time he hit me
    I knew things had changed.

I hated the way he walked,
    The way that he talked
And I despised the way he said
    my name.

And I vowed that from that day forward-
    My love for him would be no more.

# My Heart Would Surely Bleed

To know what you really think of me
My heart would surely bleed

The things that you think I've probably done
The places you  think I've been
The kind of person, you think I am
I'm right, you really don't know me

Despite what I try so desperately to show you
You seem to think I'm a sneak- a liar
      a person that can't be trusted
      deceiving you with every move I make
      pursuant in ruining your life

I love you 'til death, and even after
But who cares
      no you
      and why

Because once upon a time
A young girl slipped
She fell and bumped her head
The bump, it rose and gave her pain
And you believe she thrives on the ache

My heart would bleed
I know it for a fact
And shortly my soul would be dark

I-Love-You, my love
Believe what you will and do
But there is one thing you need to remember
Incessantly against me, we fail

Darkness hovers above your head
Only you possess the sword to cut through it
Unbelief and mistrust you'll not let go
So let me go- that seems easier for you
Just let me go
And be happy

# Not Long Ago

It seems like not too long ago
We were laughing and talking together
You made those funny faces, while explaining
Even while hurting, instead of complaining

I dreamed of you last night
That I saw you again
I had one more chance to tell you that I love you
All I need is one chance to be sure you know I love you

I heard that you smiled when the angels came for you
That you even laughed when they said it was time
So, I guess it's okay that God ended your life
Now there's no more pain, or grief or strife

It just seems like it wasn't that long ago
That we prayed to and thanked God together
You still sang to him with a voice that wasn't supposed to be
Now you can sing to our God in perfect harmony


In memory of Vivian Martin-Sunset June 18, 2004

# Out of Control

Spinning, spinning, spinning, spinning
Out of control
is
my life
Out of control
is
my life

I have
no control
of
my life
I have
lost control
of
my life

Tossing, tossing, tossing, tossing
my soul
can't find relief
I can't
breathe any more
my soul
can't find relief
my soul can't
find relief
my soul can't find relief

# Pain- Untitled

It's sickening to live this incessant cycle
        Of confusion, heartache and pain
To be a woman
        Making the choices of a child
To dream of love
When there's no one to fulfill

It's tiring to cry this same pool
        Of unnoticed tears
To feel weak and helpless
        While trying to appear to others strong
For your heart to burn
        As the fire seeps through its cracks

To feel like giving up the fight
To feel like letting go
To hurt so much you can not cry
To fear what you do not know

# People Are Dying Everyday

People are dying everyday
    Some not knowing why

A boy walks out the door unsuspecting
    And is stabbed in the heart
        He's dead

A girl is simply with her boyfriend
    And is shot by mistake
        She's dead

People are dying everyday
There is pain, grief, and sorrow

Mothers are crying for the children they've lost
    And children are seeking for their parents

He is alone without his brother
    And she cannot live without her sister

People are dying everyday
    The Lord is coming soon.

# Sometime Lady

You remember, don't you
The way I kissed you
And touched you
And held you close
When forever was all that was on our minds
And eternity was not long enough...
You still want me, I know
I see you stare
At the lips that once kissed your brow...
Voluptuous, aren't they
These lips of mine
True givers of pleasure they are
And I see you reaching
For the curves of my hips
Longing to be their guide...
You've forgotten, have you
How you turned away
Neglecting,
Abandoning my love
Thought you'd come around
Every now and then
With the pain
That only I can heal...
But no more, I say
Can you taste of this nectar
So rare and so sublime
I can not be
The sometime lady
To a man
Who won't be mine

# Take A Look

Look into my eyes,
Tell me what you see.

Do you see the pain,
      the sorrow, the emptiness?
Or do you see happiness,
      laughter, and joy?

Look into my heart,
Tell me what you see.

Can you see the loneliness,
      the hatred, the heartache?
Or can you see love,
      comfort, and peace?

Do you see?
Can you see?
To understand ME
You MUST take a look.

# The Song

There is a song of love
      Of Joy
      And Happiness too,
A  song that has vanished within my heart

There is a song of hatred
      Of loneliness
      And sadness too,
A song that has formed in my heart.

For when I sang the love song,
      My heart was broken to pieces.
My feelings were hurt
      And I was pushed so low,
The song of sadness was my savior.

# To Be Alone

Is it really so bad to be alone
With no one to tell you
How lovely you are
And no one to hold you
when your heart's been broken...

You watch the others
The girls with their lovers
Envy, jealousy,
even hatred
floods your body...

And questions enter
inside your brain
Why?
When?

...Is it really so bad to be alone?

# To Die There

If you let them
>People will put you where you don't really belong
>In a place where darkness always prevails,
>Heartache is rampant, and sadness incessant

To lie there, to cry there, to die there- forever.

If you are not careful
>Your comfort will come from the depths of hell
>Fresh flowing blood will be your warm blanket
>Screams of terror your lullaby
>And pits of darkness your bed

To lie there, to cry there, to die there- forever.

Don't be too satisfied with what you have
>Your house can turn into a place of captivity
>Your lover, a mirror of hatred and mistrust
>Your day, a pool of sorrow for you

To lie there, to cry there, to die there- forever.

Sooner or later
>You will feel the spread of emptiness inside
>Feel the conception of misery within your womb
>Your eyes will find rest on that thing called nothing

To lie there, to cry there, to die there- forever.

To lie there
>  With your pitiful self
>  Feeling sorry for yourself though you have everything
>  Your eyes too clouded to see all that's good

To die there
>  Because now it's too late
>  Too late to change what you could have before
>  Too late to be where you really belong

Forever.

# Where Were You

When I searched for love
and could not find it,
Where was your heart
to join with mine...

When I shuddered and shivered
from the cold glares of others,
Where were your arms
to comfort me...

When my soul was empty
like the seat beside me,
And I searched for someone
to share my time...

Where
were
you?

# You Know Me So Well

I'm glad you know me so well
It's really nice
It's nice to now what I'm really saying,
      whenever I tell you my thoughts
It's nice to hear where I've really been,
      whenever I come home
Yea, I sho' am glad you know me so well.

I'm glad you know me so well
It makes me happy
It makes me happy when you read my mind,
      and tell me things that I didn't know
It makes me happy when I kiss your  lips,
      and you ask me who else I been kissin'
Yea, I can't get over
      how glad I am
      that you know me
      so so well.

# Passion

# Can You Feel Me

Skin to skin and cheek to cheek
We rock softly to our own loving beat
Hand to hand and hip to hip
We dance the dance of two lovers

So tell me, can you feel me
The beating of my heart against your chest
The warmth of my breath speaking in your ear
Can you feel me as I gasp in fulfillment...

Head to head and ear to ear
We sway gently to our song
Thigh to thigh and toe to toe
We write a melody of our love

So tell me, can you feel me
The tingling of my skin as you touch me lightly
The flutter of my lashes on your neck as you hold me
Can you feel me as I sigh in my pleasure...

# Eternal Embrace

I think it is not the fact that we are...

It is the heat of our bodies
     Mixing together
The beat of our hearts
     Pounding so closely

I cry.
     Not because we are...

It is the pleasures that you give me
     Your lips on my skin
The joy it brings me
     Your loving hands

You're loving me
     Holding me
     Caressing me tenderly...

In an eternal embrace.

# Faithful

Faithful to me
      You say you want to be
            But I know the needs of the heart

The heart needs love
      The heart needs loyalty
            My heart needs affection you can't give

Faithful to me
      You say you want to be
            But I know the needs of the mind

The mind needs trust
      The mind needs sweetness
            My mind needs peace you can't give

Faithful to me
      You say you want to be
            But I know the needs of the body

The body needs tenderness
      The body needs care
            My body needs caresses you can't give

Faithful to me
      You say you want to be
            But you can't supply my needs

# How Do I

How do I contain the passion inside?
The feelings of warmth at the thought of your kiss
How do I explain these feeling within?
The frantic beating of my heart and the tingle that runs
up my spine

That God has graced me with your presence
And created a love so genuine and sweet

Beauty and peace lie deep in your touch
Your blessing of kindness has opened my heart

How do I cope with the thoughts in my head:?
The thoughts of kisses, and laughter, and joy
How do I cure this plague in my mind?
The sickness in my stomach, when you're not here

That God has renewed my faith in love
And created a hope for completion

Rapture and ecstasy in the harmony of your voice
Paradise I find in your arms.

I...

A kiss...

A touch...
A moan from deep in my throat

A sigh...
A groan...
A whimper escapes my lips

I...
I want...
I want you...
My sweet

A word...
A whisper...
A tickling inside my ear

A look...
A stare...
A bond between you and I

I...
I miss...
I miss you...
My love

Hold me...
Caress me...
Say those words I love to hear

Let me...
Baby...
Do all the things on my mind

I...
I need...
I need you...
My sweet


Wanting...
Yearning...
Longing the face of my love

No sleep...
No rest...
Only when you are with me

I...
I love...
I love you...
My Love

# Sweet Temptations

We make small talk about the events of our past
And I'm tempted to kiss your lips to stop the pain
　　　　To stop the pain that flows from within them
　　　　　　　and erase all the hurt that they whisper
I'm tempted to touch your soft, tight skin
　　　　To smooth away the hurt that it's felt
How sweet it would be to hold you in my arms
　　　　From dawn to night and night to dawn
　　　　　　　never letting go 'til you ask

We talk quietly of the desires of our hearts
And I'm tempted to open myself up to you
　　　　To welcome you inside of every part of me
　　　　　　　and enjoy the sweet pleasures of your company
I'm tempted to offer you my heart, mind and body
　　　　To stroke and caress as you please
How sweet it would be to unite with your essence
　　　　To make it a part of my own
　　　　　　　and savor the fire ignited

We share with each other the emotions we'd hidden
And I'm tempted to hand over the key
　　　　So you can unlock the passion that waits
　　　　　　　and release all the love I can give
I'm tempted to reveal my true identity
　　　　And allow you to see what is real
How sweet it would be to stand before you unveiled
　　　　To be loved without secrets
　　　　　　　With no secrets to my love

# Tell Me

Tell me why you love me
   or even why you care
Tell me why you  caress me
   And kiss me right there

My  mind is racing
   And my heart is pounding
Tell me why I'm breathless
   And longing for you

Tell me why I want you
   and why you're always on my mind
Tell me how I please you
   And what you really need

My body is tingling
   And I shiver with delight
Tell me what this feeling is
   And will it last all night

Tell me how you know my heart
   And the desires I'd locked away
Tell me why I'm euphoric
   And weeping with ecstasy

My lips await your kisses
My body awaits your touch
Tell me the answers to all of my questions
Tell without saying a word

# This Passion

I can't fight this passion inside of me
This feeling is overtaking me, defeating me
I'm filled with desire uncompromising
It runs thru me like the blood in my veins
I long so desperately just to feel your kisses
They cling to me like dew on morning grass
Igniting a fire burning deep within me
Consuming every thought, dream and feeling...

I can not battle this passion from within
So intense that I ache at the thought of you
I'm filled with desire that's oh so strong
The emotion suffocates my very soul
I long despairingly to hear your voice
A melody so perfect, only God could write
The pounding is so fierce from within my chest
My heart loses rhythm, when I think of you...

I can't keep wrestling with this passion
So weakened by the lingering scent of your skin
Desire saturates my complete existence
A mere drop of your love leaves me gasping for air
And I long incessantly to have you near me
Your essence engulfs me as though it were my own
A mind altering excitement pulses thru me
Intoxicating are the dreams of possibilities of what you
and I could share...

# When I Close My Eyes

When I close my eyes at night to rest
I hear your voice-
      Like a melody
A song that only I can hear
Especially when I feel you near

When I close my eyes at night to sleep
I feel your lips-
      Like treasure seekers
Searching the plains of my neck and shoulders
Claiming territory not encountered by others

When I close my eyes at night to dream
I see us together-
      Like two lovers
Arms linked in a simple embrace
Side by side staring out into space

When I close my eyes at night, you see
I open a world for you and me

# When You Turn Out the Light

What do you hear
     When you turn out the light
          and the darkness envelopes your body?

Light whispers tickling your ear, and
Tiny spurts of joyous laughter?
Can you hear me calling you, calling out your name?

What do you feel
     When you turn out the light
          and the darkness envelopes your body?

Small kisses above your eyelids, and
Smooth caresses upon your skin?
Can you feel my sweet, sweet lips touching lightly upon
yours?

What do you dream
     When you turn out the light
          and the darkness envelopes your body?

Two people hand in hand, and
Dark bodies linked as one?
Are you dreaming the line of my figure, only belonging
to you?

When you turn out the light, tonight
     Will you be thinking of me?

# You Called Me

You called me, called me to come
    Come to you
        In the middle of the night

You asked me, asked me to stay
    Stay with you
        All through the night

I walked out, walked out to you
    Coming to you
        In the middle of the night

I answered you, answered your plea
    Staying with you
        All through the night

Our lips touched, touched so soft
    Softly we kissed
        In the middle of the night

Our bodies mixed, mixed together
    We became one
        All through the night

# You Like That, Don't You

Whispering softly
       in your ear
Telling you how much
       I want you near
You like that, don't you
       Yes, I know
And if you wait for me
       I'll make it so

Kissing you lightly
       upon your lips
Guiding your hand
       to the curve of my hips
You like that, don't you
       Yes, I know
And if you call for me
       I'll make it so

Touching you gently
       about your skin
Saying I love you
       Again and again
You like that, don't you
       Yes, I know
Save your love for me
       And I'll make it so

# A Few

# Extra Beats

# 2 Different Birds

Two different birds
    flying in the same path,
Neither knowing where their wings
    may bring them.

Two different birds-
    Dependent on each other.

For one is small,
    and weak,
    and fragile,
The other is big,
    and strong.

Two different birds
    have seen more than all.
These birds have traveled
    far and wide.

Two different birds-
    Dependent on each other.

# Black & White

You  see black
>     And she sees white
>     And he doesn't know, they're all the same.
Where shall I go?
What shall I do?
No one here can care for me...

Because,
>     You see black
>         And she sees white
Children can't figure out they're all the same.

# Flower Boy

Slowly,
He touched the petals
So lightly and gently
He caressed their softness

Others were talking,
Yet he was silent
A song he sang
      to the flower he held

Slowly,
He twisted the stem
Up and down
He ran his fingers
Careful not to bruise
      its greenness

Others were laughing,
Yet he was silent
Loving words he spoke
      to the flower in his hand

# I Stand Before You Naked

I stand before you naked
Completely exposed
Nothing left to hide
Nothing left to hold

Revealing to you what few have seen
My flaws, my mistakes, my scars
Sharing with you my deepest possessions
My pain, my heartache, my love

I stand before you naked
Not a thing have I hid from you
Nothing left to surrender
Nothing left to give

Vulnerable again to rejection
What if what you see doesn't please?
Shaking inside from fear
What must you think of me now?

I stand before you naked
My mind an open book
With nothing left to protect me
Tell me, what will you do?

# I Want to Write

I want to write something
I'd like to write something
Something is on my mind

So many thoughts
So many feelings
So many things surround my spirit

I want to write of love
I want to write of hate
I want to get these things off my mind

Passion's on my mind
Agitation's on my mind
A storm keeps forming in my head

I want to write something
I'd like to write something
Something is on my mind

# Life

I held it for a moment,
     Only for a moment.
A moment to see the light
     And then to see the dark.

I held it for a moment,
     Only for a moment.
A moment to see there's love
     And then to see there's hate.

I held it for a moment,
     Only for a moment.
A moment that was short,
     But a moment there still.

# Life Can Be So Hard

Life can be so hard
      When there's no one there to help.
Life can be so hard
      When no one seems to care.
When I look back
      And think things over,
      I realize that I've had it good.
Sometimes I've thought
      That I'm all alone
            But then I realize I'm not
Life can be so hard at times
When you don't know what's going on.

# My Road

I know it like the back of my hand,
      The yellow veins,
      The black blood,
      The scars and scratches upon its surface.

My road-
      The road I live on
The road I run
      and creep
      and crawl on.

I know its language
      The sound it makes
         as it sleeps at night
      The crackly laughter
         as I tickle its stomach

With my feet
as I run
on
my
Road.

# My Time

As I walk through the forest
       early in the morning,
The forest floor wet,
       and glistening from dew,
My saddened heart finds joy,
       in the songs of the birds.
My dark soul brightens,
       with the beauty of dawn.

This is my time.
A time to myself.

To shake off that burden,
       that weighted my shoulders.
To throw away bad memories,
       that pounded in my head.

This is my time.
A time to myself-
       of temporary happiness.

# Out of Control

Spinning, spinning, spinning, spinning
Out of control
Is
My life
So, out of control
Is
My life

I have
No control
Of
My life
I have
Lost control
Of
My life

Tossing, tossing, tossing, tossing
My soul
Can't find relief
I can't
Breathe anymore
My soul
Can't find relief
My soul can't
Find relief
My soul can't find relief

# Outside

I see people sleeping,
and walking and talking
Patches of brown
Patches of green
I think I see a horsefly
      or is it a bird
         or a butterfly
This rug is alive
      with ants and such
I hear it
      something grinding
      something roaring
      sliding, flipping
The smell of food
      my stomach growls
The wind is blowing
      lightly moving the tallest of the grass
Dogs barking
Cars and trucks
The sky is  pale
      As though it is sick
What makes a sky ill?
The clouds that float around its face?
      Or maybe the stars that come
         when the sun goes home...
Pounding and crashing
Grinding and groaning
And screeching and screaming
Little birds sing
      But you have to listen closely

A lonesome boy
      with hardly a friend
Could I be his friend?
Yes, but he doesn't know
I watch him
      Observe him
I even try to walk
      the dark corridors of
          his mind
A light shining
      but the day is here
Her red hair blows in the wind
White birds fly in the sky
Grass has built up around
      the pole
Little ants crawl in the cracks of the walk

# Talk to Me

Talk to me
Let me hear your soul
Tell me what's on your mind

Tell me your dreams
And what your heart desires
So that I may begin to fulfill

Talk to me
Let me hear your heart
Tell me what's in each beat

Tell me your feelings
And any hurt
So that I may soothe your pain

Talk to me
Let me hear you speak
So that I may begin to provide

# The Tree and Me

Sitting alone
> Among these people

He and I
The tree and me

He restrained
> Cut and pruned
>> Forbidden to yield the beauty
>>> That's inside

My heart confined
> Torn and broken
>> Forbidden to show the love
>>> It can give

Speaking silently
> But no one knows

He and I
The tree and me

I see his limbs
> There, but not fully

He sees my hands
> Free, but shackled

Surrounded by a world
> With so many masks

We both long
> To leave ours behind

He and I
The tree and me

# Track

The frantic beating of the heart...
The heavy breathing so hard to ignore...
The cries of pain...
The feelings of regret...

What else can you expect?
But the passion of track...

# What Right

I know you may find me
different and abnormal YOU may even find me cruel.
What right do you have
to judge me so?
Have I wronged you in some unknown way?

I know you may find me
        heartless and careless.
YOU may even find me conceited.

Different and abnormal
        I may be in your eyes
Heartless and careless
        I will also accept.

But cruel, I am only to those I despise,
Jealousy, makes you say I'm conceited.

What right do you have
        to judge me so?
Forgive me for whatever I've done.

# Woman- The Animal

What is the most
        beautiful animal?

It is woman

She purrs when she's
        stroked
And cuddles
        like a bear

She can see her man
        a mile away
And smell his cologne
        after he leaves a room

Woman-
The most beautiful animal.

# Woman- The Dog

She can be man's
      best friend
Or his closest enemy

She comes when he
      calls
Picks him up when he
      falls

When she is betrayed
      She leaves him alone
He wakes up one morning
      and finds she's gone

If you feed her
      and pet her
      and give her love
She's a friend 'til the end
Or another man's love

# Woods

Protective arms stretch high
        above me
Shielding me from the anger of the sun

The bushes talk
        and gossip to each other
"Look at those clothes she's wearing!"

My feet slip slightly
        as rocks roll away
Frightened by the pounding of my feet

The weeds bite
        and gnaw at my legs
Trying desperately to slow me down

I run
        and I slip
        and I dodge
        and I turn
The woods are my enemy-
        My joy

www.ingramcontent.com/pod-product-compliance
Lightning Source LLC
Chambersburg PA
CBHW022024170526
45157CB00003B/1348